SCHIRMER'S LIBRARY OF MUSICAL CLASSICS

Vol. 153

CARL CZERNY

Op. 139

One Hundred Progressive Studies

Without Octaves

For the Piano

Revised and Fingered by

MAX VOGRICH

G. SCHIRMER, Inc.

DISTRIBUTED BY

Hal•Leonard®
CORPORATION

7777 W. BLUEMOUND RD. P.O. BOX 13819 MILWAUKEE, WI 53213

100
PROGRESSIVE STUDIES
without Octaves.

Revised and fingered by
Max Vogrich.

C. CZERNY, Op. 139. Vol. I.

4.

Allegretto.

5.

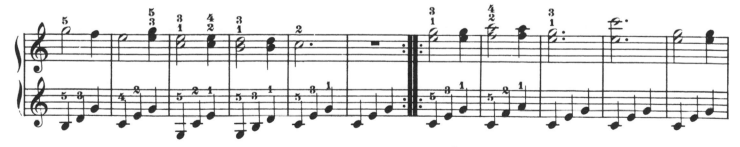

6. Allegro vivace.

7. Allegretto.

Allegretto con moto.

8.

Allegro.

9.

Allegro.

12.

10343

Andantino.

16.

10

Allegretto.

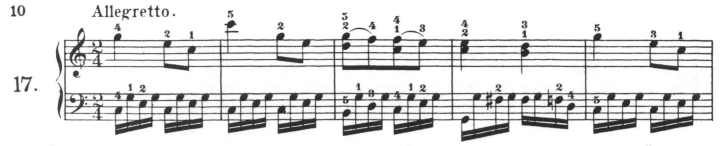

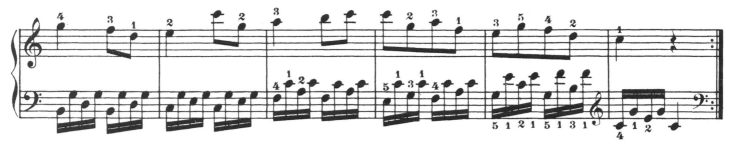

Allegretto.

Allegro.

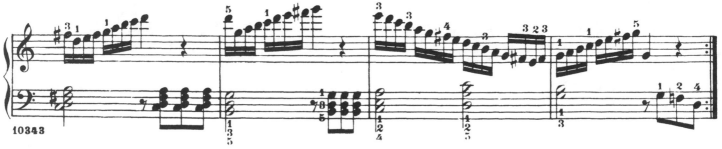

10343

20.

Moderato.

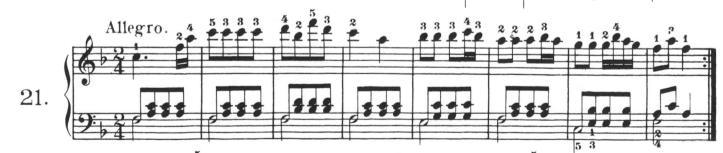

Allegro.

21.

12

Andantino.

22.

Andante.

23.

Allegro.

24.

Allegro.

25.

26. Moderato.

27. Moderato.

28. Allegro vivace.

Allegro, quasi presto.

29.

Marcia. Allegro maestoso.

30.

Allegretto vivace.

31.

Allegro moderato.

32.*)

*) The pupil should be able to play the scales fluently in all the keys, if he is to derive full benefit from the following more difficult pieces.

33.

10343

Andante espressivo.

34.

Allegro moderato.

35.

36. Allegro veloce.

37.

38.

39.

40.

Allegro molto.

41.

Allegro comodo.

42.

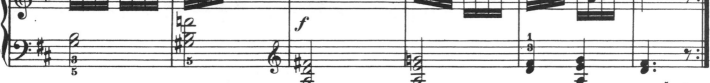

43. Allegro.

10343

Andantino.

47.

Allegro vivo.

48.

pp *leggiero.*

sempre **pp**

Moderato.

49.

p *dolce cantabile.*

cresc. *dim.*

50.

Moderato à la Marcia.

52.

Vivace.

55.

10343

Allegro moderato.

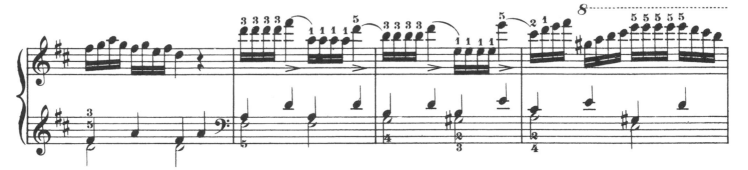

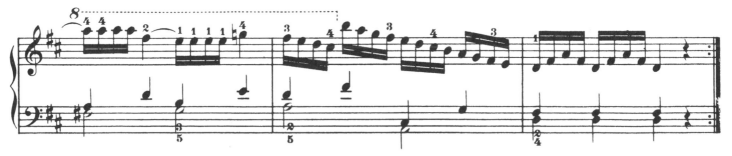

Allegro vivace.

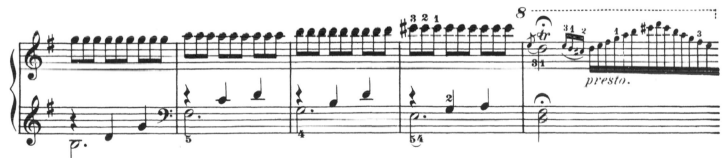

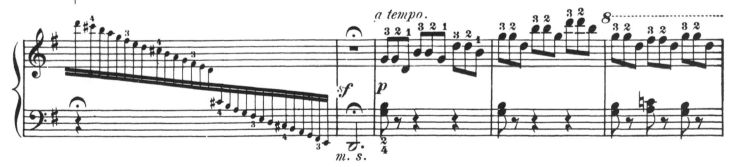

Andantino con dolcezza.

60.

Allegro.

61.

100
PROGRESSIVE STUDIES
without Octaves.

Revised and fingered by
Max Vogrich.

C. CZERNY, Op. 139. Vol. II.

Andantino con moto.

62.

Allegretto.

63.

Allegretto vivace.

64.

Allegro vivo.

65.

Lento cantabile.

66.

Allegro.

67.

Allegro moderato.

68.

40

Moderato.

72.

p $dol.$

p $dol.$

✢) Ped. (Pedal) means that the foot should press down the damper Pedal, until directed by the proper sign (✳)
to release it.

Moderato, quasi Andantino.

73.

Allegro moderato.

74.

Allegro vivo energico.

75.

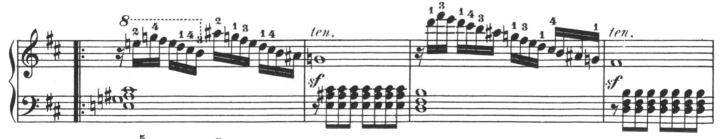

The pupil must play the following scales, without the notes, daily; and must recite to his teacher the number of sharps (♯) or flats (♭) in each, at every lesson.

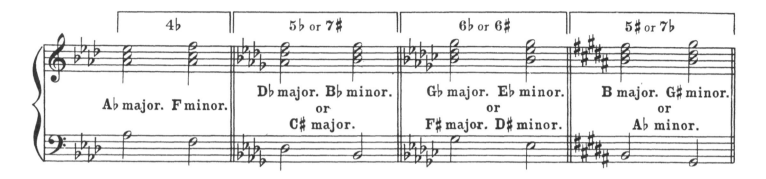

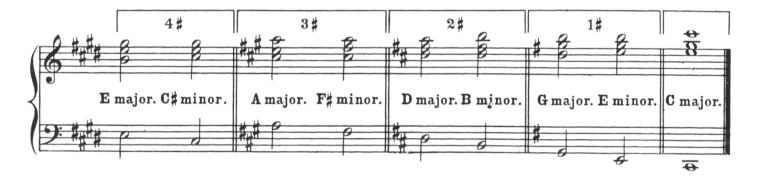

Allegro vivace.

77.

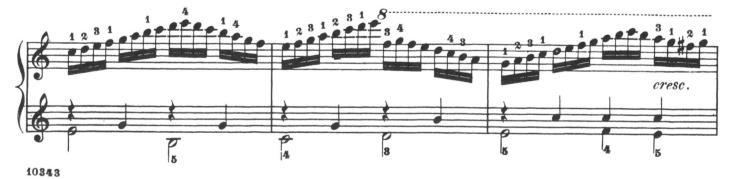

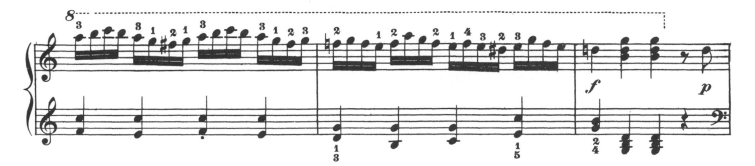

10343

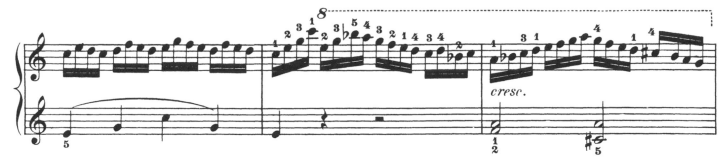

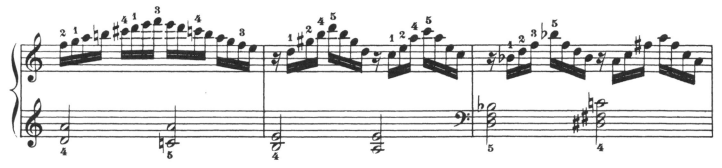

10343

48

Andante espressivo.

78.

Andante espressivo.

79.

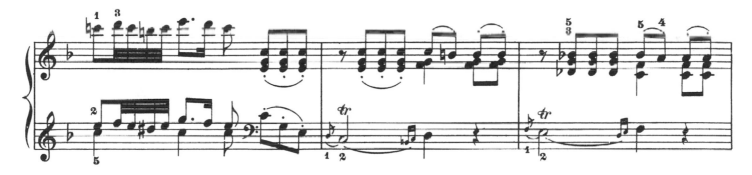

80.

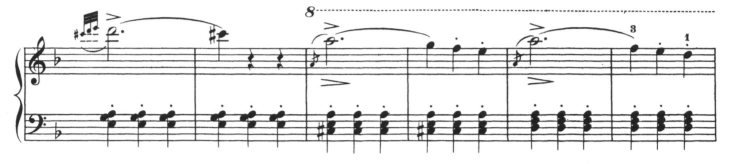

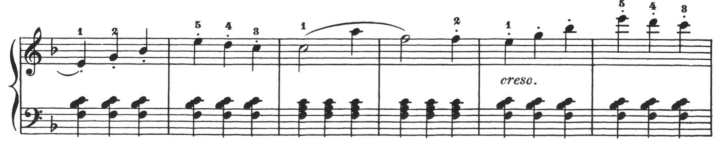

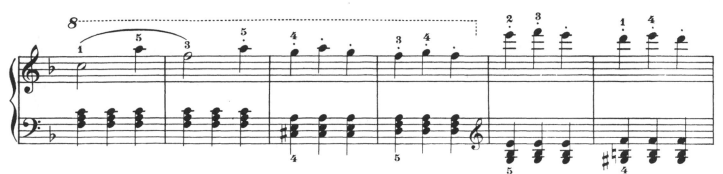

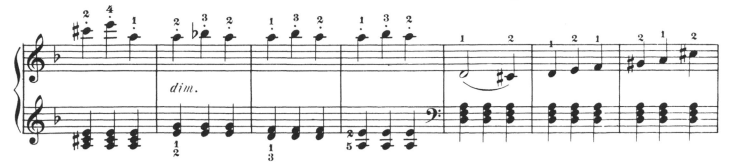

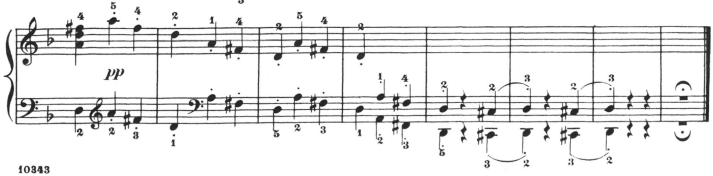

10343

Allegro vivo.

81.

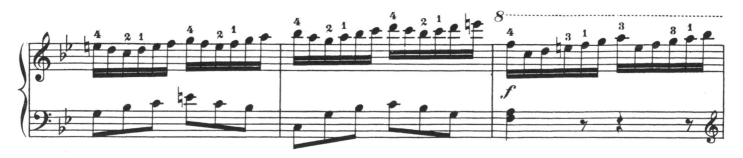

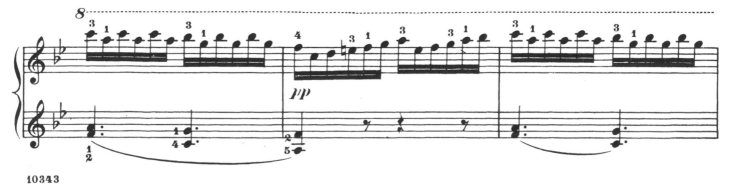

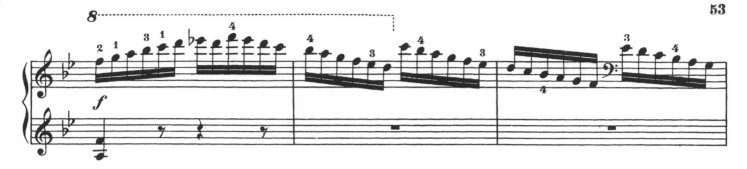

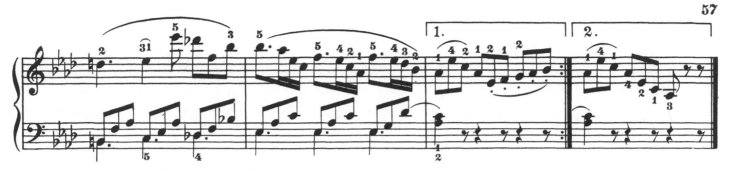

Allegro marcia.

86.

legato sempre.

10343

Allegro con moto ed espressivo.

87.

Allegro molto.

88.

Andantino.

90.

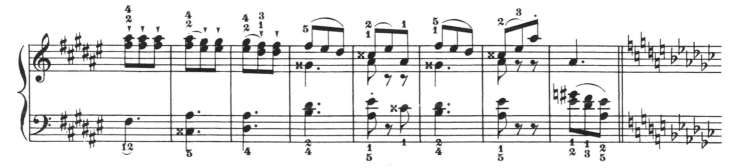

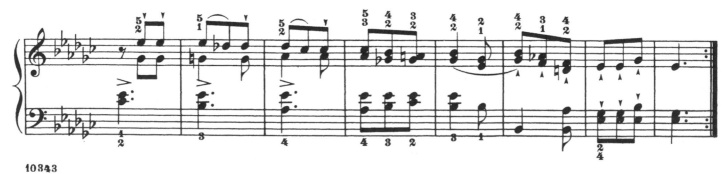

91.

Allegro.

p leggiero e scherzando.

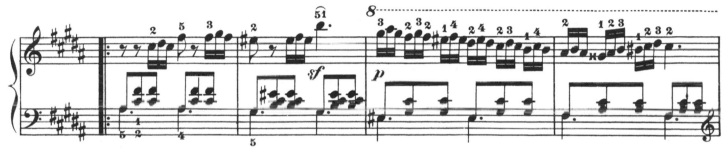

10343

Andante à la marcia.

92.

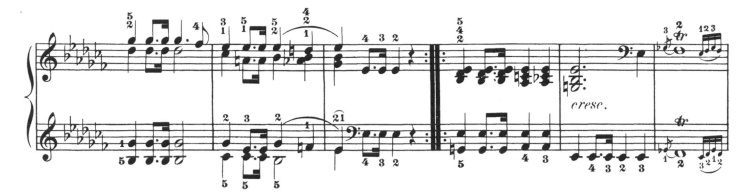

Andante grazioso ed espressivo.

93.

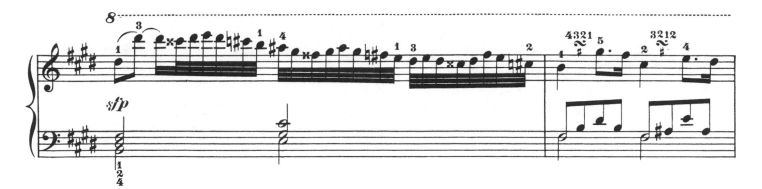

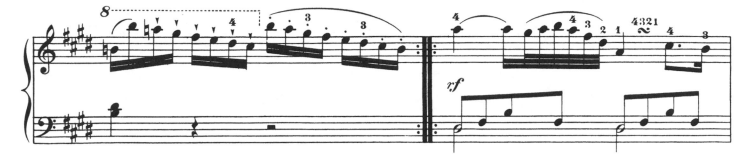

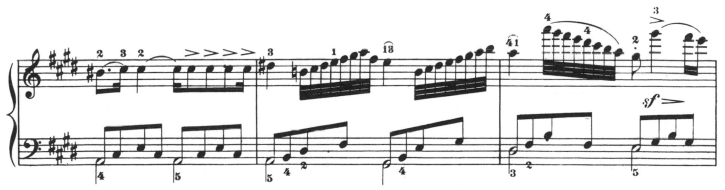

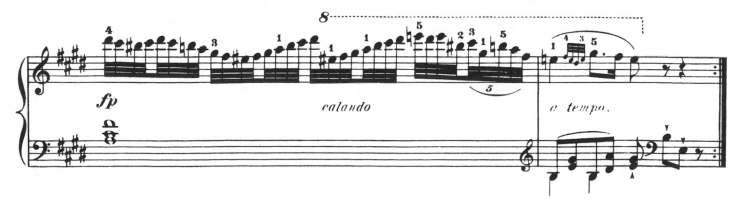

10343

Allegro molto.

94.

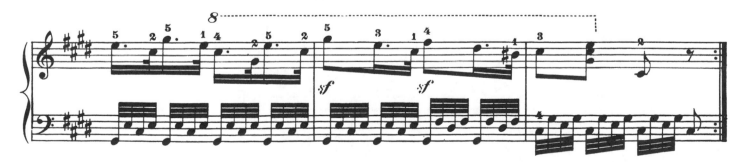

Allegro.

97.

p *leggierissimo.*

cresc.

f

Allegro.

98.

Allegro molto, quasi presto.

99.

Presto.

100.

p leggieriss.